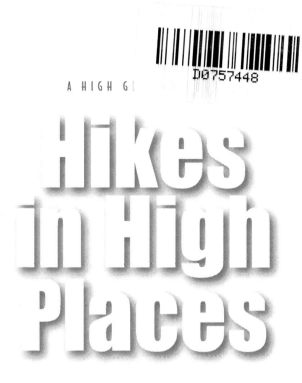

A HIGH G|

Hikes in High Places

Transforming Hikes Atlantic/Pacific

Bill Rozday

Virgin Pines Press
Frederick, Maryland

HIKES IN HIGH PLACES
Transforming Hikes Atlantic/Pacific

Bill Rozday
Virgin Pines Press
Frederick, Maryland

Copyright 2015 by Bill Rozday
Published by
VIRGIN PINES PRESS
6671 Seagull Court, Frederick, MD 21703
www.virginpinespress.com

The author or publisher assumes no responsibility for the impact of
any outdoor-related activities undertaken in response to this book.

Printed in the United States of America
First Edition April 2015

Book Design by KarrieRoss.com

Publisher's Cataloging-in-Publication
Rozday, Bill.
Hikes in high places: transforming hikes
Atlantic/Pacific/Bill Rozday.—First edition.
pages cm
Includes index.
LCCN 2014935164

ISBN-13: 978-0-9664875-5-8
ISBN-10: 0-9664875-5-9

1. Hiking—United States—Guidebooks. 2. Natural
history—United States—Guidebooks. 3. Mountain plants
—United States—Guidebooks. 4. Mountain animals—
United States—Guidebooks. 5. United States—
Guidebooks. I. Title
GV199.4R69 2014796.51'0973
QBI14-600052

To my California friends —
for open spaces and open minds.

Other Books by Bill Rozday

High Ground
Peak Hikes of the Mid-Atlantic States

High Ground II
Hiking Appalachian Topographic Culture

High Ground III
Freedom Hikes

High Places

They are called hills, summits, benches, plateaus — all of them high in relation to the earth surrounding them. Often, their physical context determines whether we call them bluffs, overlooking water; or summits, overlooking land; and always, their surroundings contribute to their distinctiveness. On one we walk atop volcanic glass from a lava flow; on another, we walk on the sand of an ocean dune.

Their elevation and latitude contribute to their unique botany and geology, and our culture shrouds them in philosophy and art. For thousands of years, people have looked up at high places and wondered. In this book, we wonder with them.

The instinct to seek high places surfaces in the creation of major hiking trails on both the Atlantic and Pacific coasts. In North Carolina, the route of the Mountains-to-Sea Trail extends from summits of purple rhododendron to the crest of a huge sand dune, with 530 miles currently complete. In California, the Bay Area Ridge Trail traces the high ground above San Francisco for 340 miles and will total 550.

When cultures that succeed us look for evidence of our lives, they will look upon our trails as socially progressive. On the tablelands or escarpments where native Americans once traveled and traded, we walked and thought and planned our complex society along ribbons of packed earth, and in the process gained perceptual separation. — Medicine Bow Mountains, Wyoming

July 2014

Elevation 9640'

Contents

Hikes in High Places

Bluff

TOFINO, BRITISH COLUMBIA

(Nuu-chah-nulth Nation)

Horseshoe Cove Ferry from North Vancouver, British Columbia; cross Howell Sound; Nanaimo; Route 19; north 26 miles; Route 4; west 97 miles; then north 12 miles to trail sign.

Where the trail breaks from forest to ocean, a dark rock formation, its dimensions indexed to the height of the tides, rises above the Pacific, softening itself in pine needles and evergreen salal (*Gaultheria shallon*) blooming white in July. Behind the orange indian paintbrush (*Castilleja miniata*) fringing its grass-carpeted edges with brightness and First Nations sunset legend, evergreen cones appear on the ground in the shadows as the rock mounts to a party of huge Sitka spruce trees, virgin evergreens, centering a 1-acre plot above the bright marine space.

One tree, waist-wide, extends a welcoming low limb as a perch above the surf noise. In the elevated garden surrounding it, a Rufous Hummingbird (*Selasphorus rufus*) flies by over the salal flowers, or a dark Bewick's Wren (*Thryomanes bewickii*) offers his song, lively as ocean surf, counterpart to the thoughtful trills of the Varied Thrush (*lxoreus naevius*) behind the beach. Looking back to the sandy shore from this perch, the bluff rises.

Back down to the base of the rock, the Pacific crashes and wets the walls and orange and purple starfish cling to mussel beds. Spring-green sea urchins brighten the pools. The maritime abundance of this place folded this rock island into a busy First Nations village before Europeans had any notion that either village or rock existed.

Back ashore, then upward to the overseeing shoreline bluff, European and First Nations culture coalesce. Their collective thoughts join beneath Sitka spruces (*Picea sitchensis*) that make a statement grand as that of the ocean itself, attaining dimensions that class them with arboreal chiefs such as redwoods and sequoias.

This gateway entity of the British Columbia coast occupies the Long Beach unit of the federal Pacific Rim Reserve. Called Schooner Cove, it enfolds brightly painted wooden houses comprising a First Nations community overseen by a Sitka spruce community. The trail ascends a bank into trees that truly guard, more than mere markers or symbols, towering into the blue, their bases looming in the shadows like mossy cliffs.

Pacific Coastline

These trees among trees, approaching 300 feet in height and 50 feet in circumference, rise from a shadowy history. The First Nations people living alongside on their lands known as Esowista offered sanctuary for the giant spruces through their tribal claim extending from the Pacific inland to the present-day coastal road that runs through Christmas wreath-dense greenery. The bluff formed their backyard, with their homes so close to the towering trees that a falling trunk would land among them. Again, genetic memory likely lays a claim, reaching so far back that it contains this forested bluff as a barren glacial heap washed by waves that receded for centuries after the glaciers melted, granting today's sandy beachfront of the village.

Over the ages, the trees grew in peace, protected in their isolation. When Europeans began to colonize Vancouver Island, the Sitka spruce grove survived due to the lack of any use for Sitka spruce wood. The establishment of the Reserve in 1970 conferred further protection on the ancient stand and also exiled chain saws from the management plan for the bluff. Park personnel studied the ecology of this high ground and affirmed its basic value, with specialists like ecological scientist John McCormick finding evidence that wildlife used it as a crucial travel avenue.

Sheltered by the huge trees, the ancient marine village began to reassert itself through population growth at the beginning of the 21st century. Possessing rightful title to the adjacent lands, the residents of Esowista negotiated with the Canadian government over an expansion of their settlement, with the elevated bluff presenting a tempting site for development.

As the parties to the negotiation conferred, the successive circumstances that set the trees apart from our ambitions extended themselves into a hybridized resistance to settlement. This resistance arose from ancestral respect for the giant trees on the bluff, combined with modern ecological regard for them, and it spared the spruce stand in an unprecedented melding of diverse thought. The Esowista residents agreed to locate the village annex on a site removed from the bluff, along the beach in a protected nook of expansive Schooner Cove. Now, thousands of people from all over the world walk an elevated cedar boardwalk trail and glimpse the First Nations village below the huge tree trunks.

On the shoreline bluff, intellect uncovered limits of the concept of property and in the process allowed human values of respect to firmly embrace the First Nations people of Esowista. The tree trunks lead like long arrows to our thoughts, surmounting the fragmented tokenism of European-First Nations relations to an old and straightforward dialogue with nature and ourselves.

Carry a raincoat on this hike, because Schooner Cove receives 120 inches of rain annually — cool rain, mild rain, windblown rain, with the birds singing on through it.

CHAPTER 2

Dune

OCRACOKE ISLAND, NORTH CAROLINA

(Woccocon Nation)

Kitty Hawk, North Carolina; NC-12; south 71 miles;
Hatteras-Ocracoke Ferry; NC-12; south 8 miles to path
at bridge.

I t's a path of the people, more significant for its informal personality than physical qualities. Four parking spaces around a brush-shrouded bridge constitute its link to the world. It falls into the roadside vegetation with no discernible objective, running for no more than 100 yards. In an age when everything in America, including paths, seems to be catalogued by some agency, its very existence is remarkable, particularly in the midst of a governmentally administered place like Cape Hatteras National Seashore.

Its identity is ambiguous. The path defines the boundary between off-limits bird sanctuary north

7

and south. The density of the surrounding brush and the 100-degree summer heat distort its extent, amplifying travel along it into a greenhouse journey. It probably existed before the bird sanctuary was instituted and earned the honor of its continued presence through a respect for tradition of the natives on Ocracoke Island, where it runs about 4 miles north of the village of Ocracoke itself.

As a traditional trail, it assumes the most direct route tenable; and its unpublished status spares us the typical environmental disruption that surrounds hiking paths. It cuts deeply into a dune, enforcing an uncertain peace with the encroaching poison ivy and greenbriar and foreclosing collateral paths. It's strictly a travel route; yellow beach flowers bloom unmolested along it. That many of the people who use it are naturists tends to promote gentle treatment of the flora.

Tourists have used it for 50 years at most — from when Route 12 came to Ocracoke Island. Yet, topography and forestry combine here to create a natural trail foundation that may have led early islanders and First Nations people to take advantage of it. It ends at a break in the dunes, so demands no climb over the fragile sand barriers. A marshy channel flanks it, so canoeists and fishermen no doubt made use of it over time.

Scrub growth, among it yaupon (*Ilex vomitoria*), weaves a stabilizing foundation beneath, maintaining the dune that it crosses at one point. Yaupon not only provides durable terrain but a dependable source of nutrition through its boiled leaves, which yield a black, vitamin-rich tea.

It's not that people did not walk on Ocracoke in early times. The desolate ocean here drowned 99 steamship passengers that islanders streaming over on foot laid to rest beneath the dunes north of the path. One sunstruck evening, a lady in a traditional skirt walked toward the ocean as I stood there offering a greeting that she disregarded. She turned left and walked northward toward the burial sites and I forgot about her until I followed the path back to the parking lot and saw no car there to connect her walk with reality.

The yaupon that grows where the trail crests the dune likely grew here before the highway came. A type of holly, it bears the holly trait of long life. Each year that its roots spread under the sand, it builds more permanency into the dune supporting the path. Here, yaupon began to fashion a sand dune following retreating surf and a drop in the salt content of the atmosphere, probably subsequent to an attempt by the Atlantic to cut through to the low ground of the creek.

Yaupon becomes a 100-year-old shrub. The toughness that it exhibits in its hard, evergreen leaves, together with its habit of spreading by long roots and thereby persisting if damaged, allows it to linger for an indefinite time after withstanding the initial challenges of colonization in a salt-laden environment. A resident of Atlantic Beach, owner of a nursery, points to yaupon of large dimensions that he saw as a child 60 years ago. They grow in the heart of yaupon range, along Route 58 south from Atlantic Beach, where formal hiking trails lead through a community of large specimens.

Striving to knit the sand together so that a stranded man or horse can climb above ocean level, yaupon stands welcoming, its leaves shining in the summer heat; on the gray winter beach, soothing with a green promise of fresh tea, trying to build history out of pale sand. Take its life-giving leaves and rest on its high ground.

Follow this trail carefully and avoid freelance forays into the thorny, textile-consuming shrubbery.

CHAPTER 3

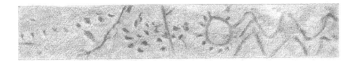

Sand Ridge

MERRITT ISLAND NATIONAL WILDLIFE
REFUGE, FLORIDA

(Timucuan Nation)

*Titusville, Florida; exit 220 from I-95; State Road
402/406; Max A. Brewer Causeway; SR 402; Visitors
Center; SR 3; north 2 miles; trail sign; dirt road to parking space under Longleaf Pine (Pinus palustris) tree.*

Oak trees of one species or another form
a great forest in eastern North America that
runs like a wave for well over a thousand
miles, breaks near the Florida line, then dissolves in
a 5-10-foot-high ripple further south in that state.
The ripple, known as the Florida scrub, seeps away
with a rich constitution of Sand Live Oak (*Quercus
geminata*), a species that achieves a height of over 10
feet here but typically grows head-high. Its leaves
and acorns assume a similar form as those of classic

live oak (*Quercus virginiana*), which grows where the arboreal wave begins to break further north.

The ripple runs up onto a shore of saw palmetto (*Serenoa repens*), which it incorporates as a forest understory. In horticultural terms, it consists of a dense landscaper's line, any portion of which could be broken and lifted onto the front edge of a townhouse lot, trimmed flat and watered. When home lots displace this type of forest, bulldozers scour it away, with no chainsaws needed.

On Merritt Island National Wildlife Refuge, within thousands of undisturbed acres, a trail traces high ground through the Florida scrub. It goes on for 1 mile, following a sufficient acreage of scrub to offer one of the few realistic chances to sight the endangered Florida Scrub Jay (*Aphelocoma coerulescens*). The footpath is known as the Scrub Ridge Trail.

This low-slung forest possesses ground level life that disturbance, whether by bulldozer or transplanting, destroys. An initial representative of Florida scrub is a crawling cover of gopher apple (*Licania michauxii*), an evergreen herb sought after for environmental landscaping due to its soil-firming ability and useful fruits it bears. Large and fragrant, the fruits perfume the air from yards away with an alluring sweetness.

This forest has a keeper, a reptile living at ground level called the gopher tortoise (*Gopherus polyphemus*). At 12 inches, it is the largest land turtle in the East. It functions as the primary architect of the Florida scrub, creating a system of burrows that accommodates a number of native species. It works through the sand, creating habitat for snakes, toads, insects – as it eats its favorite food, gopher apples.

At head level, the Florida Scrub Jay maintains this forest. Able to live nowhere else, the marine-blue jay, bluer than the common Blue Jay (*Cyanocitta cristata*), feeds on the Sand Live Oak acorns and perpetuates their growth by distributing them over the sandy ground. Only around 8,000 members of this species survive, all within the state of Florida. They are part of a traditional ecosystem, its integrity sustained by its density, which affords little if any niche for alien life.

If the Florida scrub is the dissolution of a wave, then the shell mounds are the dunes, the silent keepers of history and repositories of distant influences that washed up at undetermined times. The original human inhabitants of Florida, living as agents of nature, contributed this high ground to the landscape and in so doing maintained the integrity of tropical natural history on the islands of the southwest Florida coast. When the Calusa people consumed whelk and conch meat, they discarded the shells, creating heaps that sometimes reached over 30 feet in height — bumps of relief on otherwise unrelieved flat topography.

These shell heaps are the original home of Florida citrus. Either through self-propelled boat trade with tropical islands, where the Calusa spread the seeds of fruit they obtained; pioneer citrus plantation stock gone wild; or native flora finding refuge on these undisturbed archaeological reserves, citrus historically associates itself with shell mounds. They preserve the legacy of the early citrus industry by displaying the natural fruit that preceded our cultivated varieties. Sour orange (*Citrus aurantium*), a miniature replica of commercial oranges, grows there, and key lime (*Citrus aurantifolia*). Papaya (*Carica papaya*) with its big leaves maintains the tropical theme. Players in a retrograde global economy introducing a range of foreign plants to Florida, our native predecessors left a means to preserve our heritage in their shell mounds.

The mounds attract a variety of classic Florida plants. Their dominant tree, gumbo-limbo (*Bursera simaruba*), reaches 50 or more feet in height, with an unmistakable reddish trunk. Where oaks colonize these mounds, they create soil that wild orchids relish for its well-drained position above the sand.

Captain Brian Holoway, authority on the natural history of the islands of southwest Florida and owner of Captiva Cruises, walked with me down the beach of Cayo Costa Island, situated across the water from the community of Captiva, and explained how he has made the shell mounds a focus of tourism and long-term object of study.

By extracting information on history, whether human or natural, from these structures, he feeds the interest of tourists searching out a local angle on the Florida outdoors. Tourists come from diverse places to southwest Florida and offer diverse perspectives in their queries about the only elevated topography in the region.

We walked into the cabbage palm-Seagrape forest that controls the flat terrain of the island. Brian talked about how the elevation differential offered by the shell mounds allows individualistic species with less spreading potential to survive. On Cayo Costa Island, the differential reaches 18 feet at its greatest. That level enables the growth of royal poinsettia (*Euphorbia pulcherrima*), which creates a reddish trail visible from a low-elevation plane flight. It is the defining plant of this island's shell mounds.

Like the island itself and the shells on its shore, this plant came from the ocean, though exactly how is a matter of conjecture. The sea currents function like the winds of a mountain forest in transferring plant seeds, with a species native to Cuba such as this poinsettia able to travel with seabirds or storms to the white sands.

In the 1700s, Captain Holoway explains, Latin fishermen maintained camps on Cayo Costa, probably locating them near the landmarks of the shell mounds and possibly gracing them with their native poinsettia or spreading their seeds. 200 years later, a small village located on the island likely featured poinsettia, introduced formally in the United States in the early 1800s, as landscaping. The mounds either preserve the record of personal presence, or possibly support a relict native population of a plant not officially recognized as indigenous to Florida.

The scrubby, the discarded, the forgotten — in a state intensely altered, beautified and given endless attention in a kind of landscaping strife, this is where history and natural integrity retreat to. With the legacy they conserve, such places become symbols of something higher.

Diamondback rattlesnakes inhabit the terrain along the Florida Scrub Trail. Carry mosquito repellent, since the extensive marshes nearby constitute a breeding ground.

CHAPTER 4

Headlands

MENDOCINO, CALIFORNIA

(Pomo Nation)

San Francisco, California; CA-101; north 85 miles; CA-128W; 55 miles; CA-1N; north 10 miles.

When I first recognized it, I realized that Mendocino Headlands Fragrance had the power to restore. Senses weakened from a 2 a.m. drive into a black Northern Pacific emptiness, I stepped into the early April morning as the sun, cresting the hilltop town behind me like crystal, touched a Headlands wet with spring dew. The remarkable diversity and density of grasses breathed a self-sustaining fragrance — not mower-induced, but offered freely. Each step was a distillation of Mendocino Headlands.

In keeping with this unexpected quality, the Headlands are counterintuitive in their relation to the town itself. Closest to the Pacific, they supplant the expected villas and cottages with an empty expanse of grass. Nearly half of a mile inland, the grass ends at the furthest extension of Mendocino's halted progression of wood palings.

Framing my walk was perhaps the most glorious landscape on Earth, created by a Pacific Ocean that asserts its presence constantly. Sea arches lend a ragged contour to the frame. To the south, to the north, to the west, the aquamarine waves rush through them, wetting the deep green kelp covering the rock. At one point, the sea pierces the Headlands itself, surging 50 feet below the grass through a hole that redwood (*Sequoia sempervirens*) loggers used to slide tree trunks through to a waiting ship.

Over countless ancient mornings, complex geology achieved the tremendous table of earth here on which we work out a scheme of botanical cooperation. It involved change so deep and broad that it overcame the ocean itself. Before the redwood forest that once cloaked the Headlands yielded to the settlements that took advantage of their high flatness, it was a wet slab of sand washed by tides.

The slab disappeared beneath the ice of a continental glacier, which maintained it in a position above the water by lowering the sea level around it as it took up the saltwater into the glacial structure. A powerful earthquake then elevated the table further, far enough upward that subsequent glacial melting left it above the rising sea level, in the sheet outline that the ice pressed.

First Nations people appropriated the headlands along this segment of the Pacific coast as a fishing grounds. North of Mendocino, a projecting table of land lies with vegetation nearly polished away from their footsteps as they prepared their mussel and abalone harvest, a steep mountainside behind them and beneath them the surf.

The fragrance of the Mendocino Headlands is a result of a giving back and forth between nature and man. As Portuguese farmers tilled the land, they created space for native grasses to flourish freely and convey April through their fragrance. Wildflowers such as yellow poppies and indian paintbrush accompanied the grasses and maintained a dialogue with the sun. The Portuguese also brought Mediterranean grasses with them, which seeded themselves and mingled with the native grasses, bringing European comfort to the migrant farmers.

Chinese settlers maintained plant relations that transferred themselves to the Headlands. Above Portuguese Beach in April, the yellow-flowering kale the Chinese introduced brightens the foreground of the town portraits that photographers shoot.

The Headlands remained a zone of open grass because the Mendocino founders avoided the Portuguese immigrants farming the soil, unaware that nature was cloaking such prejudice with an exemplary prairie. As the redwood shacks of the newcomers deteriorated, the land fell into disuse and the county acquired it. What started as class exclusion eventually led in 1974 to the inclusive designation of State Park for the 347-acre Headlands. Now, the strong ocean that carried diverse people to Mendocino exerts its influence through the prevailing winds blowing inland from the ocean, knitting exotic and native grasses into a prairie grass library.

At Mendocino, on possibly the most picturesque high ground on earth, we meet and look now. The logging and farming and ocean harvesting are through. Much as the land settled itself after an earthquake lifted it, our culture has rearranged itself. It has settled into a diverse community of painters, photographers, poets that parallels the ethnic diversity that drew upon this land. The paths they follow run through the grasses of the most magnificent cultural backyard in America.

Since this is a high-latitude hike, the weather often remains cold and windy into late April. Combine the walk with a visit to sheltered Portuguese Beach along Main Street or dinner in one of the gourmet restaurants.

CHAPTER 5

Clay Cliff

MARTHA'S VINEYARD, MASSACHUSETTS

(Wampanoag Nation)

Woods Hole, Massachusetts; ferry to Oak Bluffs, Martha's Vineyard; 45 minutes; car rental; 20 miles; Aquinnah; trail runs for .5 miles beginning at the Aquinnah Cultural Center signpost, ending at the beach.

On Aquinnah Cliffs, one of the last casual places remaining on the frenetic Atlantic coast, an old wooden Cape Cod house surrounded with weeds overlooks thousands of miles of blue. Through the blackberry thorns and over the cliffs, a nude beach wears the badge of low-key living.

It is also one of the few remaining authentic places. Unaware tourists see pure Cape Cod in the pink roses filling their digital frames; but the typical Cape Cod roses, *Rosa rugosa*, originated in China.

The true Cape Cod rose, *Rosa carolina,* colonizes remote places, such as a blueberry-studded hillock overlooking the marshes of the Wellfleet Bay Wildlife Sanctuary; and here at Aquinnah Cliffs, in this nature sanctuary managed by the Wampanoag Nation, undisturbed by the driving regimentation of East Coast life.

In June, the hiking trail at Aquinnah Cliffs is an unkempt tangle of abundance. The pink of the wild roses ascends thickets of blackberry blossoms and fresh wild grape leaves.

The Wampanoag revere this high ground. "High clay" might be more appropriate — clay that symbolizes the human link to nature. Red and white, the clay arrived via glaciers pushing it, along with smooth granite boulders and sand, to the ocean itself, which carves the cliffs from it. The Wampanoag instead carved decorative clay bowls to hold their wild blueberries.

The elevated terrain recently factored into a landmark court decision establishing the primacy of the Moshup Trail, which leads to the Aquinnah Lighthouse, in relation to building lot access, denying easements for home construction along the route of foot travel. The acreage encompasses a rare ecological zone known as northern heath, home to distinctive plant and bird species.

On this high ground stands the oldest native Baptist church in America, dating to 1693. At its base runs America's oldest nude beach. The Wampanoag embraced Christianity but never embraced shopping mall swimsuit shops and real estate developments.

CHAPTER 6

Coastal Mountain

ATLANTIC HIGHLANDS, NEW JERSEY

(Lenape Nation)

New Jersey Turnpike; Exit 11; Garden State Parkway; Exit 117; NJ 36; south 10 miles.

Mount Mitchill in Atlantic Highlands, New Jersey is a hill of healing today. At 266 feet above the fresh water of the Shrewsbury River and branch-cut blueness of an Atlantic Ocean view, it offers the highest ocean vista along the entire mid-Atlantic seaboard. It drops off with an abrupt profile created by the altering process of slump blocking, during which fragile sands and clay drop from its resistant underpinning of ironstone, increasing its pitch and scenic scope. On September 11, 2011, smoke rose through its tree trunk vista, across New York harbor, as this seaside hill oversaw an attack from a culture thousands of miles distant.

The oak trees and mountain laurel bloomed on the Mt. Mitchill summit for millions of years – crusade-free millennia preceding an attack that diminished its seaside vista. America reached into its past on 9-11, from where it began to heal. Now, on the top of Mt. Mitchill, we commemorate our tradition of resistance with a replication of the high ground natural history that precedes us and will outlast us all.

Surrounding a huge limestone eagle sculpture commemorating our response to the attack is a clearing. The opening symbolizes the sun-struck emptiness following 9-11. Joseph Sardonia, head of landscaping for the Monmouth County parks department, directed the planting of humble Sweet-fern (*Comptonia perigrina*) and Hay-scented Fern (*Dennstaedtia punctilobula*), two emblematic species of high ground botany, in a formal garden here. Ever anxious to colonize the most vulnerable places, whether a barren ridge bereft of good soil or a fresh cut left by the falling of a tree, they stand there in the full sun and offer their aesthetic peace. Their fine fragrance hanging in the searing heat shows the melding of the gentle and strong that comprises free culture.

The ferns were planted to represent the inception of a healing journey, the fragile graces that the mind grasps as it finds reality after a wound. Their fronds waved here on the acidic ground before the days of colonization. They preceded our lawns;

the Lenape tribe, who left humble disarray of soil as archaeological evidence of their presence on this hill, would have welcomed them as they looked out over the ocean from behind the sassafras and oak and the laurel flowers that still brighten the shadows in June. During long journeys, sweet fern tea found use among the natives as a strength-giver.

From this piece of high ground, the Lenape could make use of the clams and fish they harvested from the Atlantic shore in a place away from the wind and harsh sunlight of the sands. Their lifestyle demanded less travel than was typical, because here on this estate of sorts, they had the natural wealth of both the marine environment and the hills.

Joseph Sardonia looks at the Mount Mitchill summit and plans further landscaping medicine. He foresees a secondary stage represented by American Holly (*Ilex opaca*) shrouding the carpet of fern while permitting its continued existence, much as adulthood overlays childhood.

This second layer would be permanent, symbolic of the long and slow life of the holly trees in this ocean-tinged environment. Within sight of the vista, directly across the harbor from Staten Island in the Gateway National Recreation Area, stands Sardonia's prototype forest, a stand of ancient hollies with an understory of fern, growing with an almost personal willingness to sustain itself in poor seaside sand.

Beneath the ferns of the hill is an underpinning of ironstone, an indomitable rock formed from iron deposition beneath gentle ocean water. The stone provides cultural footing, in that it went into the manufacture of armaments by British soldiers who struggled with us for possession of the hill, eventually abandoning it in defeat.

Now, the stone memorial eagle centers a terrace engraved with the names of Monmouth County patriots who died battling terrorists, its talons grasping a twisted beam of iron from Ground Zero. The talons grasp as well the iron armaments of the defeated British and the fern-clad ironstone of the summit.

We responded to 9-11 with earth-based ideas on this high ground. They are thoughts of connectivity – willful, health-giving — feminine ferns and masculine iron merged. Such concepts sustain nations.

Combine this hikelet with a day at the beach at Gateway National Recreation Area, which spreads over the scenic view below.

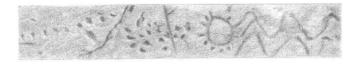

CHAPTER 7

Sea Hill

TOFINO, BRITISH COLUMBIA

(Nuu-chah-nulth Nation)

Horseshoe Cove Ferry from North Vancouver, British Columbia; cross Howell Sound; Nanaimo; Route 19 - north 26 miles; Route 4 - west 97 miles, then north 14 miles to spur road and parking lot.

Radar Hill is a different kind of beach walk, and an old one. This is a place of resistance. The ocean crashed against its base for millions of years without altering it. A glacier rolled over it, leaving only scratches visible today. Whether in its prior form as seaside outcrop or current form as Radar Hill, it remained timeless amidst a procession of great geologic events. It establishes and holds an initial interior point, segregated from its marine origins by a freshwater creek running 450 feet beneath the Pacific view it offers. Its rock constitution drops steeply, so steeply that a trail

31

leading to the beach offers ropes lying alongside as aids in the descent.

This trail commences in a steeply pitched place of dark evergreens, a near-vertical forest with huge trunks, then plunges down the rock faces using available fissures, breaking into an imposing rainforest. The knee-high roots of red cedar trees block one step, knee-deep muck captures another, a knee-high log the next. The path seeks hard for a tenable route through forest where mountain lions lurk. It only runs for a half-mile; yet, it leaves even athletes sore-muscled. It is an insulting breed of beach path, no stroll down the dunes but an exhibit of coastal solitude created by roughness. At its terminus, flat sand scrubs the foot obstacles away as surf noise fills the evergreens.

Radar Hill itself rises up into deep shadow and silence. A dense stand of western hemlock covers it just as eastern hemlock covers the eastern high places. The jade-green forest nation advances vigorously toward the nearby seashore, while seashore life fades back from the approaching green, leaving it largely silent. A solitary sound, melodious but untraceable, rings out amidst the hemlock — a Varied Thrush, much like the Veery (*Catharus fuscescens*) of the Appalachians in voice but offering whistles along with its flute-like tune. In the background, the ocean roars and fog drifts.

Where a parking lot breaks the shadow, Steller's Jays (*Cyanocitta stelleri*) maintain one of the basic man-bird relationships, looking for offerings from the few naïve enough to pursue some seagull-type association with the beach here. The vast scope of rugged country this jay inhabits, into the interior ranges, lives here in this bird of shadowy brown-blue.

The Steller's Jays of 2008 may be the descendants of the Steller's Jays of the 1940s accepting food from soldiers. At the crest of Radar Hill, the Canadian Air Force installed a radar battery during the Second World War — new technology meeting old high ground. In this silent place, signals other than the perpetual Varied Thrush song and protective of the entire Canadian interior ran through the air. Here, the ears of a huge nation poked through the graceful evergreen boughs that symbolize it around the world as Canada expressed its collective resistance on this resistant rock structure.

The spectacularly unalterable rock comprising Radar Hill is known as greywackie. It possesses something of the ocean's permanence, having solidified from the gray sand under the waves into its cold grayness. A primordial cement comprised of sand and small stones, it resisted the ocean's erosion because it arose from that ocean. Nature, unable to grind it flat, clothed it with a dark forest and left it overlooking an uncivilized valley that presents a fragment of mountain scenery at seaside from the ancient view afforded here.

Because it resisted the forces that conspired to smooth and homogenize it, Radar Hill leaves us a place of awareness. It yields a view, yet apprises us of threats. As soldiers or as tourists, we are stranded here on this problematic rock stage, dark and silent, this room laid out for listening and looking, as we feed blue jays for diversion.

The ocean below signals the season with the spouting of migrating gray whales beyond the hemlock branches. They send a message from California that spring is approaching, and we pick up the silent spouts with binoculars.

Carry a change of clothes with this hike, because the rough footing leads to a lot of squeezing through and detouring, while the beach itself is a rugged one bordered by rock and rain typically falls.

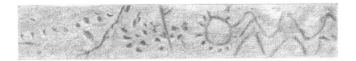

CHAPTER 8

Foothill

HAYWARD, CALIFORNIA

(Ohlone Nation)

CA 580; Castro Valley Boulevard; 1 mile; Lake Chabot Road-2 miles; small lot upslope from paid Lake Chabot entrance.

Behind Castro Valley, California, a city of hillside streets, rise hills with a different identity: hills of a bordering nature, pale and barren like an eloquently fashioned wall, bereft of even the most minor straggling house or road. I climbed atop them into their grasses and felt within me the gravity of their border.

These San Leandro Hills, part of the California Coast Ranges, are the initial high ground beyond the Hayward-San Leandro earthquake fault line lying silent in the flat town of Hayward spread out beneath their grassy rim. They wrinkle and pitch with the look of violence that has ceased, covered over.

Perpetual strife beneath them, hikers on Fairmont Ridge look upward. On America's western border, the old Atlantic grayness behind, they leave their own border marks.

At the base of the ridge, in the city of Hayward itself, a juvenile correctional institution stands within the earthquake fault zone and its incipient wedge of destruction. Overseeing its violent divisions with peace, a monument to children killed by violence crowns the hill. Rows of symbolic trees, one planted per year, rise behind the polished granite.

Eucalyptus Trees–California Coast Range

The full view of San Francisco, altered by bay mists, stands in the distance below the overseeing clarity of the hilltop. In the bay, wartime threats echoed in a military post perched above the hilltop eucalyptus and later abandoned as reason transcended conflict. Here on this restful patio of land, we watch the fog and fault lines.

We leave our marks and look upward. Their natural habitat thousands of miles away, some of the first eucalyptus trees brought to America took root on this hill in the 1860s. Tall and white-trunked, a row of them occupies the crest. With no forest to accompany them and only sky above, we made the eucalyptus row the fragrant border of the cities of Castro Valley and Hayward. Beside them runs the cart tracks of a pioneer road now supplanted with the prints of caring thoughts. Beneath jet fuselages, the eucalyptus row runs as a window-seat landmark on the San Francisco-Washington, D.C. flight path.

The bent pockets of hilltop hold memorials. Across the narrow ridge line from the grassy rim above Hayward is the grassy overlook of Lake Chabot; standing amidst the summer brown is a bench dedicated to a hiker who regarded the lake below from this view before crossing the border of this life.

The signs we leave on the land are often borders, and borders denote the value of things being divided. The gold grasslands of these California Coast Ranges look across the San Francisco Bay and an old world left behind across the Pacific, on their crests stone walls of unknown origin. Maybe the old world left behind was one deserted by unrecorded Chinese wall-builders landing on our shore thousands of years ago. Maybe it was our First Nations peoples' old world left behind, meted out and divided into pastureland by the Spanish who transitioned from them. Along the ridgeline foundation, the earth's mass strays like broken mushroom caps picked up and set in order, the wind playing unhindered through the grass between provocative mountain and water view.

From high points like Mission Peak, where the San Leandro Hills fill out into the Diablo Range, over 100 miles of beyond, including the Sierra Nevada Mountains, is visible from the crest, a vastness that modern scientists measure as a "viewshed," an atmospheric resource.

As I walked beneath the arid sky of the San Leandro Hills, a flock of Western Bluebirds (*Sialia mexicana*) — wild, yet not wild — flitted over this free and unkempt yard of the hilltop. Not the sober illustrations in a birder's field guide; yet, not the flock of city sparrows; not the bluebirds of Appalachian legend that portended household deaths in flying against windows, they were the blue-sky border of grasses, the happy brightness of day, the healing of looking upward from a fixed point.

Golden in the April-to-November drought and green in the remaining months of winter rains, tended by cattle as they have long been between successive earthquakes, the hills behind Castro Valley are a bicolored blanket. The early settlers grazed cows and goats on this ridge of quieted upheaval, following economically the First Nations people with their hilltop hunts; now, the cattle graze for a social purpose. Today, a herd of goats advances this humble use of the hills by grazing during the season of alien grass growth, then moving on when the parks department determines that the native purple needlegrass (*Nassella pulchra*) that originally clothed these hills begins to sprout.

From the jurisdictional border of the eucalyptus trees, the owls perch in a motionless division of night and day. They leave a friendly feather on the ground and a few cries, but are only the border between what we see and what we do not. The owls gone, the day begins and the hikers in the San Leandro Hills transcend, traversing the wild and yet-not-wild lawn, within a fold of night and day, green winter and gold summer.

A hike during summer here means a hike during fire season, with regular fire engine patrols. Nearby, the Oakland firestorm of 1991, accelerated by the rugged terrain, claimed 25 lives.

CHAPTER 9

Cliff Wall

LILLOOET, BRITISH COLUMBIA

(T'it'q'et Nation)

North Vancouver, British Columbia; Route 99; east 160 miles; picnic/camping area along Seton River.

Powerful relationships proceed on the cliffs of British Columbia. Those relationships transcend our books on nature, and the peaceful salmon fishing of the First Nations people living at their base. The cliffs represent an extremity of human range.

Thousands of feet above the 6,000-foot canyon along the Seton River at Lillooet, far beyond the zone of hunters' rifles, mountain goats navigate treacherous rock faces. Cougars do the hunting up here around spectacular footholds beyond our view for the most part, unless nature stages an animal drama there for those walking the trail along the

41

river. The steepness of the rock faces reaches the extreme necessary to protect a cloud-white animal, the mountain goat, and permit a huge, tawny predator, the mountain lion, to stalk it over the accommodating tawniness of vertical rock. The mountain lion stalks us as well if we manage to scale the cliffs. They are not a place where human beings belong.

Cliffs shadow First Nations people in British Columbia. The great rock formations rising above Pemberton Meadows, beyond Whistler Ski Resort, oversee a roadside river where natives fish. A native-run filling station and cultural center look up at the 3000-foot rock wall fronting the Fraser River at the mouth of Cayoosh Canyon. At the confluence of the Fraser and Thompson Rivers, two canyons meet and a little town square in the village of Lytton vibrates with the sound of drums during pow-wows.

The cliffs offer the natives shelter from the wind and a reference to life above them, where the clouds shrouding the summits and the stream courses running from the alpine hold a reservation of wellness. Along the Pacific of their origin, the Salish peoples had looked up from water they couldn't drink to the fresh water of the alpine and the tea plants they crushed into it for flavor, just as they later looked up from the silty Fraser River.

Above the brown Fraser at Lytton, the Siska band climbed the imposing canyon walls at the

Thompson and Fraser confluence and discovered soapstone. Notably easy to carve into bowls, it affirmed belonging within their environment and gave them vessels for their teas. The canyon walls enclosed the tribespeople and allowed them to pass on a focused herbal tradition. Their geographic isolation, with the rapids of Hell's Canyon downriver and barren grassland to the north , lent gravity to their herbal knowledge.

Their kin to the west, the Lillooets dwelling beneath the cliffs of the Bridge River, still climb to a high altitude huckleberry gathering ground. These huckleberries, either owing to their particular species or the conditions of high altitude, fruit at a certain time of year coinciding with nutritional needs.

These particular huckleberries once carried a hazard to life. The berry meadows lie in a region of high ground structured in such a way that it provides a topographical entry to the barren north country of British Columbia. As such, it hosted a struggle for territory with the neighboring Chilcotin, a tribe that surged into the thin air of the meadows from the grasslands and sagebrush (*Artemisia tridentata*) to the north. Grave Valley, the Lillooets call the site of the great battle there. Only they know its location. It's up there above the cliffs, in a place sustaining, yet violent.

For the fortunate onlookers at the picnic area who might view the ancestral wildlife struggle of cougar and mountain goat on the cliffs, the performance conveys titanic power and etches itself in the mind like the nearby petroglyph etched on rock at the river mouth. They see terrain up there like a parallel earth, plainly visible, yet unreachable. If country reflects the human spirit inhabiting it, then there is ferocious power and transcendence here that eludes the First Nations people working in the Lillooet stores.

This physical strife extends deep into the earth itself — into river-drowned cliffs. A pool below Lillooet burrows into a box canyon in swirling water 1,000 feet deep. A whirlpool swings a log around and around and then sucks it under. Divers refuse recovery work when they see massive boulders rocking underwater in the relentless current.

Thousands of years removed from their migration up the Fraser, looking up at the expressionless faces of the sheltering cliffs, the natives examine their day-to-day and year-to-year lives deliberately. They develop a bodily dialogue of sorts with the teas, tracking their effects and presenting the results to the world of tourists. They live in a fixed fashion while the rest of the world hurries about filled with stress; upon that contrast, they judge the value of their clover and yarrow and huckleberry and sell them in packets in their store along the Fraser, together with carvings of soapstone.

Their tea imparts dignity to everyday plant life, to red clover, red raspberry. Look closely at the red clover plants they use and a sunset-colored abundance manifests itself. When plucked from a fresh environment, red clover breathes the scent of honey. It distills the fragrance of wild places and offers some of their essence in a packet of tea. Red raspberry leaves from their thorny and freely spreading canes carry the color of white dew from their high country. In the arid country of interior British Columbia, the shape of any leaf is the shape of life-giving moisture, flavored moisture preserved in tea.

The First Nations people will live there as long as the mountain goats and cougars carry on their parallel cliff struggles, the clover and huckleberries and raspberries grow above the rock heights and they can look up towards them. The cliff faces represent at once strife and sustenance.

A nearby creekside campground offers spectacular canyon scenery, firewood and uncrowded conditions free of charge.

CHAPTER 10

Pass

LILLOOET, BRITISH COLUMBIA

(T'it'q'et Nation)

North Vancouver, British Columbia; Route 99; east 162 miles; Lillooet, British Columbia; cross Fraser River bridge; Route 99; north 4 miles to wide space along road.

Light defines the West — bright sunlight and the pure air that engenders it. The height of the canyon walls and breadth of the tree trunks affect us in an extraneous way, but we look to the broader and greater source of light for the experience of this country, whether the Rockies or the canyonlands. It turns the black cottonwoods (*Populus trichocarpa*) of Lillooet, British Columbia into diamonds.

Maybe certain western objects would not exist absent this light simply because human eyes would fail to perceive them. A piece of nephrite jade along the Fraser River arrests our sight with a distinctive tone of green best thought of as dimensional in nature, arising from the internal crystal structure of the gem meeting the western light. Hold that jade under an office tube light and the color dies.

I hunted jade behind our cottage along the Fraser early one morning before the sun crested the canyon walls and , while I found two pebbles, I remained oblivious to their identity until days later when brighter light brought out apple-green from within black, spruce-green like poured resin. From late morning onward, the sun leads on to jade by polishing its surface with a luster absent in the flat green jasper, serpentine, olivine, chert, grossular garnet of the riverbanks below.

Nor could agate function in the hazy East. The light of the canyonlands floods the gravel bars and ignites the tiny gems with the orange fire of September grass. Even fingernail-sized agates emit this signal of light from the nooks beneath the geologic aggregations of the gravel bars. The application of sun each day to silt-covered fragments wears away this coating and assists in revealing points of light.

Light shines at the center of our existence and defines the objects most cherished to us. The universe of gemstones features much subtlety and intergrading, with quartz blending into jasper, serpentine to jade, but the light tells us instinctively what portion of that spectrum real gems occupy. This light illuminates other, profound matters.

I found my first piece of jade behind the remnants of a First Nations village, a green splinter of translucence stuck into a steep bank only yards from a grown-over Teekwillie house, underground home of the ancients. When I offered my green splinter to a friend from Peru, he looked at it and pointed out the angled break of the fragment, seeing the influence of old hands fashioning an implement.

I found two other pebbles there that year, glowing in their spruce translucence when held to the sun; over the winter, frost loosened more of the bank and sent hundreds of pebbles of varying identities tumbling out of the glacial deposit to my feet, drawing me back for more searching. The passage of vacation time wore the sharp edges from my mind and sent me into deliberate appraisal of the rocks around me. I settled into an attitude of acceptance of whatever nature offered — the crucial attitude, the context in which the ancients lived.

My mentor, owner of the jade shop in Lillooet, connects cultures with his gem knowledge. He employs a hunting technique passed on by a tribal elder: standing in a stationary position and circling outward with the eyes in a patient search for wavy-shaped stones sculpted in their metamorphic toughness rather than broken in the way of lesser stones. His is an ancient form of immersion in the environment, therapy for the hard-driving habits of sight moderns adopt.

Disarmed by the honesty of a lesson in seeing, I faithfully sought out jade, extending my quest for understanding. The process yielded the offhand reaction that caused me to place two pebbles in my pocket, a thought so casual I couldn't remember the location of the rocks, yet saw something different about them to advance my learning.

Our cottage is situated as though by Stonehenge-like alignment; indeed, the ancient Teekwillie house occupies a bunch grass-sagebrush terrace along a straight line between the kitchen window and the morning sun cresting 8,000-foot Mount Brew, turning the sage into transparent quartz in the dry air. Excavated like a fort, the subterranean site provided rest from the burning sun, relief from the winter wind, and, in the morning, the view of the river below contacting the eye immediately.

At the commencement of the September salmon run, the moon appears as though hanging only feet behind the terrace line. While I watched, a quarter-moon set there, leaving a glow behind Mount Brew after it disappeared. Many more Teekwillie houses existed here once, lost to development now but fresh to the topographically attuned mind.

People have occupied this linear alignment for thousands of years — forever, according to the tribal elders. Not lost upon the first of them, surely, was the exchanging of the orange moon at front doorstep with the rose passing of alpenglow from that mountain. Not disregarded, certainly, was the linear red of migrating salmon strung toward that doorstep upon the setting of one particular orange moon. The oranges and reds of life suffused this line of sight.

North of this terrace, the Fraser becomes an impassable canyon, but the bench elevates and continues to run. A trail perches above the river, following sagebrush and ponderosa pine (*Pinus ponderosa*) backed by the empty air of a thousand-foot drop. The sagebrush is large, up to a foot around, the ponderosa pine undisturbed by logging and permitted an indefinite lifespan by loggers who consider it too small in this northern end of its range It's a place left alone, yet a travel corridor traversed in various ways.

This path is a track of sorts, broad and open. It served as a wagon road and, prior to that, an irrigation ditch for gold mining operations; throughout, as a First Nations path for natives walking towards fishing sites, tramping along for thousands of years past the sagebrush and empty dropping away of air. A mule deer path parallels the wagon path, a railroad parallels the mule deer path, and Route 99 traces both through this high ground compromise between canyon cliffs and vertical mountain face.

The line of sight terminates at an overlook with native fishing sites far below. Upon turning around along this ancient geometry of vision, a giant piece of rose quartz glows in the sky in the evening. Mount Brew's snow dusting meets the pink of the darkening sky in the alpenglow.

The terminus of the path overlooks an unnavigable rapids a thousand feet below with waves 15 feet high, once bridged by the natives to connect an ancient salmon fishing path on the opposite bank. Salmon gather here in a black congregation tinting the jade-green outlet of a river that borrowed its name from the ancestral bridge.

Arising from an ice field 10,000 feet up in the cold clouds, the Bridge River runs through First Nations country. Its canyon walls, 3,000 feet high, burned so brightly with the initial fires of the planet that jade, tough as steel, comprises sections of them. During the glacial epoch, those ice fields advanced down the canyons of the Bridge and Fraser, picking up two jade pebbles to deposit on the terrace behind the cottage, where I saw their glacial green color and deposited them in my pocket. Relationships needn't be obvious.

Above the salmon-darkened pool at the Bridge River outlet stands the Fishing Rock, a huge pictograph painted in the 1970s by Saul Terry, local First Nations politician and artist. Executed within the circular outline of a sun disc, salmon shapes constitute its eyes and mouth. It celebrates a native way of seeing.

When Canada arrested a native salmon fisherman along the Fraser for fishing "out of season," the St'at'imc people filed suit declaring the calendar concept of season subsidiary to the natural signs of the salmon run and its offering of food to their people, winning their litigation.

There is no salmon season here, no arbitrary apportionment of time into a unit open to manipulation. There is, instead, a salmon perception. When the moon glows behind Mount Brew for a certain number of nights, it glows at the red backs of the salmon swimming northward up the river. When the light strikes a dusting of snow atop the mountain in a particular way, illuminating it like the face of a time magician changing masks, the people gather and call out in celebration.

A well-worn trail winds against the grain of the promontory overlooking the Fishing Rock, then disappears into a tract of St'at'imc land kept off-limits to outsiders out of respect for its cultural connotations. I stood there considering the outline of path among rock surfaces and then considered the treacherous ice fields above the Bridge, denied to me as well, and realized I didn't need to strive for those heights. I needed a way of seeing.

Take care to remain on the track here. The steep slope leading to the river presents unstable footing. For advice on finding jade along the Fraser River — an exasperating pursuit for the novice — contact Daniel Boersma at the House of Jade in Lillooet.

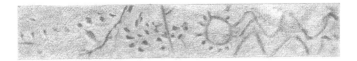

CHAPTER 11

Glacial Bench

NATIVE LANDS, BRITISH COLUMBIA

(T'it'q'et Nation)

North Vancouver, British Columbia; Route 99; east 162 miles; Lillooet, British Columbia; north 4 miles north on Main Street to Bridge River; dirt road west 10 miles to Horseshoe Bench vista.

Miles into the wilderness of British Columbia's Bridge River, the book of the landscape opens into a topographic S letter. It is nearly half a mile long, many acres in width — the ancient template of a glacier occupying a canyon slope waving ponderosa pine needles.

Walk to the edge of the tawny-colored S. The land gives way to air as though someone cut a 423-foot-deep slice away. At its base, at the fringe of the river, long-lost miners moved gravel and subsequently the gushing glacial current itself in their zeal for the gold ore here, some of the most richly concentrated occurrences of the metal on earth, leaving a sun-cleansed rock bed still visible from these heights.

In 2006, I stood atop this golden font crest, talking with a frontiersman. Transmuted across the generations by ancestral lineage and geographic singularity, George Vanderwolf casually announced that gold lay at my feet. He gestured to a line of glacial cobbles rimming the crown of the S like cake icing, marking a band of gold-producing clay into which gold ore migrated downward, left unmined as the prospectors pushed onward from this glacial flat, called Horseshoe Bench.

His family once claimed legal ownership of this vista. Wiry and tan, wearing the ever-present Canadian flannel shirt, he had overseen the building of the road that opened this canyon, had mined the gold — had achieved unrestrictedly, in a manner closed to subsequent generations and unimagined by the native generations that came prior.

He guided my gaze across the river to a faint track fossilized in the dry earth, marking the site of a waterline traversing the rock. In the early 20th century, Chinese constructed it to transport water miles over a sharp rampart of the Chilcotin range as part of their gold mining operation. It was a brief working marriage with the land, an overlay of the initial loving marriage of the First Nations people.

Vanderwolf the frontiersman began talking about the First Nations people on this crest. At a certain time of year, and for thousands of years, Horseshoe Bench has served as a First Nations mule deer hunting ground. The hunting ground is a virgin landscape of rock, bunch grass, sagebrush and ponderosa pine, the pine never logged due to its small size near the northern frontier of its range.

Nature grows trees here in a deliberate fashion, because the intermediate high ground of the bench occupies a dry zone between the moisture-gathering mountaintops and the moist cold fronts sweeping through the valleys. Some local benches see only 2 inches of rain per year — lonely places denied even the companionship of raindrops, immutable land largely unaffected by clouds.

He told me how, within the rock canyon of the Bridge River, grasses and shrubs create a remote deer world. The deer world migrates upward in the warm months, with mule deer occupying an elevation stratum of 4-5000 feet, where they find an alpine plant known as hard grass. Mule deer attain exceptional health and weight eating hard grass and then migrate downward in autumn. At the time the Lillooet tribe encounters them on Horseshoe Bench during the September-December hunting season, the fat deer graze further on bunch grass, on two species of laurel bush growing beneath the ponderosa pine, and on the alfalfa that spreads along the dirt road.

The highest elevations of the Bridge River canyon comprise an inaccessible pasture, a primary zone of greenery and coolness. The Lillooets hunt in a secondary stage of coolness and green, when mule deer fitness and the huntable weather coincide. Here in this arid outpost of the West, high ground provides life based on elevation.

The mule deer make this First Nations country. Elements of the frontier landscape, they were abundant to the extent they left big game hunters from around the world in awe, and they were free of the characteristic evasiveness of the white-tailed deer dominant in other sections of the province. The Chilcotin tribe from more northerly ground bereft of mule deer coveted their abundance and launched raids on the canyon country, killing mule deer and the Lillooets as well.

Tribal tradition places a critical sentry rock — a counterpart scenic view, if you will — directly across the Bridge River from Horseshoe Bend. From their lookout rock, the Lillooets apprehended the progress of enemy Chilcotins along their pine-studded war path running concealed geographically by the tributary Yalakom River.

Horseshoe Bench was the last of the western frontier, dominated by First Nations people, an era burning like a fire with the ashes yet remaining. Not far upstream, a short hike across a bunch grass flat leads to 100 and more stone-lined Teekwillie pits, subterranean residences lying out in the stars and sun, roofed with shadowing pine logs when occupied by the Lillooets. George recalls seeing a First Nations hunter around 1990 roaming there on horseback with his deer rifle. Here on the northern edge of the classic ponderosa pine-sagebrush frontier, that frontier never vanished, as the definition of frontier and definition of edge sustain their mutuality above the river.

The casual presence of gold in the canyon owes itself in part to the First Nations unwillingness to lay the stress of water lines and gold pans upon their marriage with Horseshoe Bench. George relates a gold mining conversation from earlier in pioneer days. The natives were familiar with gold in forms that would leave modern people feverish with lust; when asked for his assistance in working the deposits, one replied that he "wouldn't work for those yellow rocks."

The First Nations peoples' bench remains. The mule deer they won't hunt as trophies but only as sustenance still run about. Under the grasses in the crumbling glacial loam perched above the river lie the "yellow rocks" they refuse to work for just as they did in the gold rush days — in pounds rather than ounces, according to one prospector. This bench invites a fire among pine trunks for a culture whose exodus from the needle-carpeted view is disputable. The miners and hunters gone, the Lillooets can walk out through the pines on their untroubled bench and camp again in this place, stir the ashes on a piece of high ground where they treat riches casually as sunshine.

Carry water on this trek, even in autumn, due to the angle of the sun and the total lack of filtering pollution in the air. In this miners' rock Hell, the sun-heated stones burn the hands even in September.

CHAPTER 12

Upthrust Earthquake Fault

GILROY, CALIFORNIA

(Ohlone Nation)

San Francisco, California; CA-101; south 79 miles; Gilroy; CA-25; south 30 miles; Hollister; CA-146; 5 miles to Bear Gulch Visitor Center.

It was a good place for giant vultures. The California Condor (*Gymnogyps californianus*) attains a 9.5-foot wingspan and can approach 20 pounds in weight; yet, when it soars on the rushing winds, it becomes a solitary avian athlete, reaching speeds of 55 miles per hour. Climbing high on the thermal currents, into the domain of airplanes, its straightly held wings and white-marked undersides ruffle in the atmosphere up to 15,000 feet above these canyons and pines.

It was a hostile place where the dry heat immediately drew all the moisture from my nose, startling me. The vegetation stood silent, with only the sound of the dessicating wind above. Manzanita shrubs bled a maroon color along the trail beneath the condor's sky.

To the condor, Pinnacles National Monument represents a high ground reference point amidst thermal currents. As the winds rise skyward, a nesting bird flaps off of a high rock and into its hunting environment of dry air and heat, searching for the fallen animal life below. It selects the most elevated habitat, lending its own functional definition to the idea of high ground.

The condors were up there on their unique piece of high ground. This surpassing vulture species was waging a comeback in numbers on rocks that constituted an extinct volcano. The movement of an earthquake fault line transferred the volcano many miles from its origin; then, millions of years of erosion fashioned the intricate rock palace that the birds now called home – a temple of geologic struggle.

Condors inhabited Pinnacles historically, but human persecution reduced their numbers to a point near extinction, with the last recorded fly-over by a wild bird in 1987. Shortly thereafter, every bird remaining in the wild had its wildness suspended as biologists bred the condors in controlled conditions and then released them into the rock-bedded atmosphere of the California mountains.

This last sailing condor was likely AC9, Adult Condor 9, on a long-distance flight through its range searching for fellow condors. In the spring of 1987, researchers captured AC9 and subsequently bred it in captivity. In 2002, they released it in Ventura County, restoring a wilderness time clock suspended for 15 years, during which time they saved the species from impending extinction.

The place represented an isolated enclave of high ground attended by a winged high ground element. The approaching road, Route 25 from Hollister, penetrated the secluded and sparse San Andreas Rift Zone, a Mexican-like valley of heat and farms, and then found itself encroached upon by narrowing topographic walls, forcing it to slow and wind before it reached the shaded canyon floor with its gift shop and information center.

A naturalist in the rear of the center used a remote camera to monitor the progress of condor chicks in a nest far above. The birds were off-limits to visitors during this sensitive stage of life, but a ranger near a research station up in the rocks tracked condor movements, and hikers were prowling the ridgetop trying to learn of their whereabouts.

It was a day of motionless views of the Gabilan Mountains east of the Salinas Valley, a place of pause and uncertainty. There was scant green on the top of this earthquake-transported volcano's top, little in the way of life. It was a place of a powerful bird that suggested a time without the trees and fields and homes we know today. It was as though millions of empty years perched on the sandstone peaks.

Established in 1908 by Theodore Roosevelt, Pinnacles contains 26,000 acres, of which 16,000 are designated as wilderness. Over 30 miles of hiking trails traverse the resistant landscape of rock and rattlesnakes, and I stood there then along one of them, letting the distinctive surroundings reflect on me.

I searched out the meaning of the desolation. More than a National Monument but a Memorial of the Eons, Pinnacles was there long before human beings came to this Earth. It was an elevated custodian of the life that was present in this region, sending these winged emissaries to dine on the animals that died their natural deaths between these formations and the Pacific Ocean. All of this living, all of these laughing people, for these thousands of years, have not succeeded in embellishing the facelessness of this ancient crest and the death-seeking wings that soar from it.

Time your hike for morning for the best chance to view condors and avoid the debilitating heat.

CHAPTER 13

Plateau

BLACK FOREST, PENNSYLVANIA

(Seneca Nation)

PA-6; Galeton, PA; PA-44; 10 miles; Cherry Springs State Park; PA-44; 2 miles; Cherry Springs Fire Tower and Susquehannock Trail.

It was the crest of the last wild country in Pennsylvania, a symbolic inset in the narrative of the diverse core of the Appalachian deciduous forest. They were logging it up there in the blue-backed brown and gray, with synthetic machines altering its non-synthetic self; exporting corporations were investing in a place that itself exported solely the waters that trickled away and grew into the heart of great forests that stretched for a hundred miles in all directions.

I walked for a few moments through the trees and came to the sound of running water, a muted sound far over the side of the crest and deep within the trunks. It sounded like a product of the water-shed structure itself; in its faintness, as though originating above the earth in the tree branches or below the earth in the rocks.

The sound came from the totality of the water-shed crest. The existence of water in this part of Pennsylvania paralleled that of these trees, where it began to flow downhill. Within their shadow, every object, every bit of life, had a hand in producing that gurgling current. The watercourse had run for thousands of years precisely as it did today.

Deep within this huge structure, elements remain unchanged, a constancy that produces a great result of broad and clear rivers. This high place stood at the center of a huge forest; it couldn't be altered by an alien element at the distant edge, and its vast homogeneity prevented any foreign presence from expanding within it.

It remained purely northern. It represented an endless maple sugar camp too extensive to tap; the most influence we could exert were chainsaws every 100 years to take down the hard, slow-growing trunks. If an empty space appeared, covered with last autumn's brown leaves, then sugar maple sprouts arrayed themselves close to the forest floor.

Within this forest of sprouts was another forest below the level of the leaf canopy, a vast forest of Canada Mayflower (*Maianthemum canadense)* leaves.

They grew in an unadulterated fashion, not mingled with other species, in great beds dense and unsupportive of foreign species.

The sugar maple (*Acer saccharum*) foliage foreclosed the increased light that generally brightens high places. Even when the infrequent black cherries (*Prunus serotina*) were logged, leaving bare ground and debris, the maple branches spread deep shadows . With its depth, the forest enclosed all within it, including the person walking through.

Fostered by the uncompromising maple shadows, black cherry grew arrow-straight here as it shot upward to overcome the darkness, an element in a system of superlative tree growth. On the high ground of lesser integrity in Pennsylvania, red maple (*Acer rubrum*) supplants the black cherry.

Pennsylvania's nickname is Penn's Woods — Pen Woods, actually, using the Welsh word "pen" meaning "high" and adding "sylvania" for woods — "high woods," of which these are Pennsylvania's, up above 2000 feet in elevation and crowning the state for a long distance in all directions. They are high woods indeed, part of the creation which pervades us, from which we emerge and to which we return every time we hike within them.

Sam Cook, service forester with the Pennsylvania Bureau of Forestry, understands this woodland system in a particular way. This forest of sugar maple represents what foresters call an "off-site" maple stand not growing in ideal conditions, but a forest nevertheless managed not just economically but for the ecological role it plays.

These maples begin to lose their health at one century rather than the several centuries typical of specimens growing in glaciated situations where the soil contains a favorable amount of calcium. Acid rain and climate change limit this forest's growth, but its high position in the way of wet Great Lakes winds produces a high density per acre of tannin-rich tree trunks, which acidify the earth upon falling and decaying. Foresters recognize this as more than a mere maple forest and use the occasional black cherries there to further enable its existence.

The timber industry searches for advances in sugar maple culture because cutting a stand of sugar maple in this day contributes to a long-term trend known as "sugar maple decline" reflected in prices for an ever-scarcer wood product of $4-500 per thousand board feet, or roughly three trees.

Throughout most of the tree's range, acid rain and climate change work in the subsequent absence of forest cover to make the existence of a new sugar maple forest problematic. However, by looking at the totality of the forest, which includes its historic backdrop of black cherry, rather than purely its economics, we lessen this trend and keep Pen Woods alive by sustaining its resistance to change, practicing a kind of conservation by means of conservatism.

Sam Cook endorses the passive forestry techniques practiced here by noting the shortcomings of Germany's practice of consuming everything in a forest of economic value, to the point of employing wood chippers to remove every fragment from a logging operation. Studies at the Kane Experimental Forest in Elk County, Pennsylvania indicate that black cherry branches and twigs left to lay on the forest floor confer buffering protection from acid rain for a period of 50 years. Combining this knowledge with steady vigilance against fire protects this forest from direct exposure to the harsh realities of acidic precipitation and climate change, maintaining a cool and wet universe.

A mountaintop is part of the moisture itself that flows in those rivers running from these maples. The greater height of this one confers greater resistance to change upon the waters that gurgle down from it.

Directly beneath this mountaintop runs the Kettle Creek wild brook trout fishery, which withstood the negative effects of 19th century logging better than any other in Pennsylvania and became in the 21st century the state's first brook trout conservation project. The brook trout here attain larger than normal size, their backs dark like forest shadows and bellies silvery like springs running in the sun.

Pen Woods, then, will always be the state's "high woods". As long as Pennsylvania continues its practice of raising the profile of its forests among educators and scientists, this forest will remain above the wood chipping machines.

Avoid this country until June until frosty mornings and unsettled weather disappear. Even in summer, the mountains create disturbed weather. In August 1974, 6 people were killed by lightning at Cherry Springs State Park.

CHAPTER 14

Desert Inselberg

JOSHUA TREE, CALIFORNIA

(Cahuilla Nation)

Los Angeles, California; I-10E; 97 miles; CA-62E; 28 miles; Joshua Tree, California.

I drove in the dark through San Bernardino, California, then through Coachella and its renowned spring celebration, then beyond to Joshua Tree National Park, and I wandered around, jumping from one rock to another until I sat down, perching in a pile of rock rubble at 7:30 A.M. on April 11, 2014.

I had entered the desert by parking at the first trail lot on the left side of the main road through the park, about 2 miles in from the west entrance. My trail, the North Canyon Trail, runs for 1.2 miles, but I stepped off of it and scrambled up to this desolate terrace in the morning coolness.

High Desert Spring

My perch high above the canyon was essentially an eroding mountain formed of a rock known as monzogranite. Throughout Joshua Tree, there is a differential process of erosion, creating topographic relief and a summary geologic rock pile that included my temporary habitat. Rock piles with pronounced definition are called inselbergs. The disarray of Joshua Tree inselbergs merits terminology capturing the concept of "sledgehammer."

Rocks and wildflowers compete for popularity among the nearly 1.5 million annual visitors to Joshua Tree's 800,000 acres. In the 1930s, prior to its 1936 designation as a National Monument and eventual 1994 christening as a National Park, officials suggested the name Desert Plants National Park. Today, this expanse attracts rock climbers from all over the world, who consider it a premier year-round destination.

As my mind relaxed and eyes adjusted, an apricot-orange blossom appeared. It was the most perfectly formed wildflower I had ever seen among the hundreds of species I had identified on both coasts. It was a desert Mariposa lily (*Calochortus kennedyi*). It highlit a morning when I saw over twenty species of wildflowers, all new to me, in the early morning light — growing in a rubble pile.

Evidently, April 11, 2014 and Joshua Tree were the coordinates for locking me into the ideal American desert experience.

It wasn't just the desert mariposa lily. Wandering for three hours over a few hundred yards of terrain, I saw two species of large-flowered pink cactus, the Hedgehog (*Echinocereus engelmannii*) and Beavertail (*Opuntia basilaris var. basilaris*), as well as the waxy yellow Barrel Cactus (*Ferocactus cylindraceus*). Various-colored flowers, several species at a time, filled my photo frames. At times, a species called desert dandelion (*Malacothrix glabrata*) actually carpeted the ground.

This rock rubble pile is a repository of life. Wildflower seeds lie intact for long periods, undisturbed among countless crevices and odd angles of shadow. Cactus Wrens (*Campylorhynchus brunneicapillus*) burst into song at dawn, while black-crested flycatchers (*Phainopepla nitens*) perch on scrubby oak trees. The Joshua trees (*Yucca brevifolia*) themselves have grown unmolested for 700 or more years. This is a rock pile, but a pristine rock pile — hardly a place where anyone farmed or logged.

My timing was perfect. I returned to the car in the strengthening sunlight and admired a Beavertail Cactus blossom, then glanced up into the view of a snow-capped mountain through a Joshua tree branch. The roadside was filling up with cars as visitors followed me in celebrating Desert Spring.

Time this hike for the spring months in order to appreciate both rocks and flowers. In order to assure an experience with the wildflowers, contact the park at 760-367-5502 and inquire as to whether conditions favor a good blooming season.

CHAPTER 15

Escarpment

CEDARVILLE, CALIFORNIA

(Paiute Nation)

Reno, Nevada; US-395; north 71 miles; CO. RD. A-3; 9 miles; US 395; north 90 miles; CA-299; west 2 miles; wide spot on south side of road.

The Warner Escarpment is high desert on a pedestal. Rather than ascending gradually from the hot valley of sagebrush on the California/ Nevada border, the country abruptly leaps. The pedestal, built of basalt, rises above the gleam of the alkaline valley as the morning sun strikes its face in the pure and cool air. Structurally, it is a near-vertical façade left in place when the earth alongside it collapsed hundreds of feet down to form the dividing valley. It is linear high ground, sharp-sided, with a precipitous scenic view accompanying its 85-mile length. Lacking the forest cover of mountain ground, it offers an open garden moistened by winter snows.

The escarpment balances a garden of superbly drained soil studded with wildflower gems. The soil is as soft as powdered cocoa. The elements of the gems intermingle: orange indian paintbrush with gold wooly mule's ears (*Wyethia mollis*); Sierra onion (*Allium campanulatum*) with blue lupine (*Lupinus latifolius*). From the east comes a morning flood of desert light that combines with the elevation of the soil to produce a singular category of wildflower display.

The high garden elevates the plant life of the desert below into the presence of an overseeing garden plant, a plateau-filtered higher form. A mountain mahogany tree (*Cercocarpus ledifolius*) perches there on the edges of the structure, with rock and air beneath it, catching the dry sun. It curls and spreads, celebrating its freedom from the dusty, root-filled flats of the sagebrush ranches below.

The Paiute tribe celebrated mountain mahogany for its health-maintaining virtues, perhaps in acknowledgement of its adeptness at colonizing untenable footholds on the plateau edge while eking out 1,000 years of living on the rock and thin soil. The Mexicans call their mountain mahogany "wise tree" , *arbol de la sabiduria,* for its longevity and its attainment of secure perches above precipices such as this one — as a friend from that country says, living a long life in a stationary position, without exercise, through perfect adaptation to light and heat.

This mountain mahogany, together with the elemental ponderosa pine, are among the few trees standing on the Warner Plateau. The latter achieves, even with diminished dimensions brought about by the dryness, aesthetics of dappled orange bark, stout straightness and golden cones.

What remains standing of the Warner Mountains casts a rain shadow to the west that keeps the escarpment bereft of trees, which allows wildflowers to respond to the intense light of midsummer and bloom in great variety. The flat desert to the east forecloses any spread of forest onto the escarpment from that direction. The open façade of the escarpment is subject to erosion, further limiting the possibility of tree growth.

The escarpment, as a structure, is not uniform, but features many angles that either accept or reject the direct sun at a given time of day, unlike the flat valley lying under its direct rays from dawn until dusk. Wildflowers demand these angles and will not tolerate unrelenting sunlight in most cases, or the constant heat that a featureless plain exhibits. It is light that supports these flowers, angles of light and their modifying effect on heat.

The pedestal cracks at Cedar Pass, rock walls shooting up on both sides; while, at the base, wild roses grace the stones where the Paiute tribe walked yearly into their high country summer home. The route was an unchanging one transacted with the inner earth, rock enclosing it. Its deep coolness foreshadowed the coolness of their high country with its pink wild roses.

As the Paiutes walked through the crack in the escarpment, the wildflowers accompanied them with a delicacy replicated in the clean meadows. The flowers they saw are the flowers we see, because time brings no alteration to rock as it would to timbered earth. The morning coolness allows the fragile blue Baby blue-eyes (*Nemophila menziesii*) along our wayside to thrive just as the high country coolness fosters the alpine species.

Some of the flowers here are the flowers of the dry roadlessness fronting Nevada's bright emptiness, while others are flowers of coolness, reflecting the increased elevation. Cushion buckwheat (*Eriogonum ovalifolium*), lemon-yellow, spreads here, with white Dusty Maiden (*Chaenactic douglasii*). Balloon-pod milk-vetch (*Astragalus whitneyi*) opens on the uncluttered table of earth.

For several mornings in a row, I awakened near the Nevada border and, my driving hands chilly in the yet-shaded canyon, traveled west to the Paiutes' pass, following the original First Nations path at creekside and then ascending the east side of it over disused ranchland upward to the escarpment crest.

There in the midst of the searing heat of the July days, wildflowers of all colors spread out over the landscape, wildflowers of so many kinds that I expected a new species with every few steps of elevation gained.

Near 6000 feet, Oregon Sunshine (*Eriophyllum lanatum*) finds here the coolness of more northerly places for its flecks of bright yellow, and penstemon and phloxes decorate the landscape. The penstemon offers the blue sky: *Penstemon humilis* in dusk-blue. These mornings find phlox flourishing in July, with a species known as *Ph. Hoodii* carpeting the ground with white alongside a juniper shrub.

Here, an entire mountain chain dropped into emptiness, leaving blankness as commemoration, save for wildflower names reflective of linguistic emptiness. There were no European botanists wandering around in wool coats to lend their names to these flowers, so they are named for the animals that huddle beneath them or consume them. There is the luminous lavender of coyote mint (*Monardella villosa*). Jade-colored rabbit brush (*Chrysothamnus*) shelters the coyote mint blossoms.

These wildflowers are a seeding of the pure simplicity of air through which the earth fell, memorials to a cataclysm that no-one witnessed.

Before traveling here, find out whether Modoc National Forest has had sufficient rain to support robust wildlife blooms. In a good year, easily a dozen species flower here simultaneously. Free pamphlets detailing the ecology of Cedar Pass are available at trailside.

CHAPTER 16

Mountain Pass

MOUNT RAINIER, WASHINGTON

(Yakama Nation)

Seattle, Washington; WA-164 south 42 miles; Enumclaw; WA-410; east 44 miles; Chinook Pass.

At Washington State's Mt. Rainier National Park, a fog-shrouded footpath graced with deep pink Indian paintbrush crosses a high zone of hospitable footing. The elevated crossing point is known as a pass — Chinook Pass, so named for the warming Chinook winds that have accompanied those traveling it for hundreds of years. The pass is subalpine ground, the point where a storied trail, The Pacific Crest, meets a major highway, Washington State Route 410; a stone overpass securely unites trail and road.

Geography and travel routes intersect here in complete accommodation of the hiker. The path is

dedicated to the idea of high ground and offers distinctive elements not present in the low country in
exchange for a minimum of hiking effort.
Thousands of miles in length, at this juncture the
Pacific Crest is as convenient as a corner store.

The floral richness here is uncompromised — in
early July, the bright indian paintbrush, the snowfall
of Avalanche lilies (*Erythronium montanum*), the blue
lupines, the yellow Large-leaved avens (*Geum
macrophyllum*) and Pink Mountain Heather
(*Phyllodoce empetriformus*) — diverse species
blooming beside each other in a community celebration of coolness and freshness. Far beyond the dusty
sagebrush of the low country, hummingbirds dart
about for nectar in the wind and fog over blossoms
5,400 feet in altitude.

The presence of fine soil in the alpine meadows
assures that the wildflowers flourish. Contrasting
with the sharp and angular field of rocks that
constitutes the Appalachian crest and paves its
parallel continental hiking path, the Appalachian
Trail, this glacial environment benefits from the
sediments deposited by the ice sheets. The firm
earth of the Pacific Crest Trail is a ribbon of soft
brown, a corridor of uncomplicated footing among
the greens, reds and yellows.

Though not above tree line, the meadows along
the trail are nonetheless alpine in their aesthetic
constitution. Barren tree line terrain forms much of

the view, with grass among the fir trees. The indian paintbrush, light of the crest, defines it as such, showing how the native legend of its origin as sunset paint began among elevated sky views such as these.

The trail's position as part of the body of Mount Rainier lends it this alpine nature. The mountain establishes that status by extending the land elevation to over 14,000 feet and capturing the Pacific air, wetting the meadows with rain and snow, freshening the trail. The general dampness, which amounts to 112 inches per year, leaves summer snow patches at modest elevations and creates what amounts to a garden, a band of Atlantic-like lushness running through a region of western rock and sagebrush. As such, this high ground is a cultural resource in a water-deprived part of the world.

The Pacific Crest, running north-south, in this vicinity intersects the extinct line of an east-west Indian trail that originated in the sagebrush country. For a limited length of trail, moccasins and high-tech hiking boots have joined to pack the glacial ground.

Chinook Pass represents an historic common ground of diverse peoples. Tribes from both the east and west slopes of the mountain intersected each others' steps on the cultural dividing roof of the pass. They granted each other permission to wander the berry-covered boundary when in need of food for winter.

The Yakama tribe paused here on the high ground, their long path broadening, to harvest blue huckleberries spread before them in late summer, here in this cool and humid meadow room overseen by a snowy mountain curtain. They ate many of them out of hand and carried others back to the valleys in baskets fashioned of woven bear grass, which grew on the floor of the huge room essentially as baskets waiting for weaving. As they worked, the mirrors of Tipsoo Lakes reflected the den's snowy curtain and bear grass-huckleberry floor.

The huckleberries favored most by the Yakama were the species *v. deliciosum*, with a preference for this great den that the most notable occurrences of *Xerophyllum tenax*, bear grass, shared. Together with the first two grew a medicinal root, of undetermined name, that relieved cold symptoms. The Yakama gathered this last product in quantity, to fortify themselves for the months ahead when the cold would descend from the upper room to the sagebrush room of their home ground, when they would burn it and inhale its smoke. If the exertion of uphill climbing along the trail and the associated change in climate brought on cold symptoms, it offered an immediate remedy.

When the huckleberry fields became a national park, the government closed the historic den.

The snowy peak of Rainier became an iconic wilderness window for our computer screen savers, but the room of earth gifts became a sterilized containment zone when park personnel in the 1930s ordered an end to the summer berry harvests.

Yet, a certain harvest of freedom passes forward. Accustomed to a high country exchange rate of 10 miles walked for the white purity of July snow, I walked for a mere ½ mile among the wildflowers and sat by an old drift as parties of hikers filed past. Families walked past it, vacationers on lunchtime strolls, tourists from diverse places, seekers of high ground who find here a free alpine festival, a place of modern tribal intercourse as easy to attain as stairs leading up to a den.

This piece of high ground, with its sharp change in climate and mile-high elevation, demands a little physical adjustment for a fatigued person. Take a peaceful and slow hike here, resting often and enjoying the scenic delights that await with every step.

CHAPTER 17

Glacier Pass

NATIVE LANDS, BRITISH COLUMBIA

(Lil'wat Nation)

North Vancouver, British Columbia; Route 99; east 140 miles; wide spot in road immediately east of Joffre Glacier parking lot.

Grizzly country is like the country of a free-spirited man in that it offers necessary discretion of movement. There is a lot of it, but the grizzly or the man are not conspicuous within it — they use the liberty that certain terrain brings as a means to gain privacy. As for the grizzly, it roams from salmon-bearing water on the edges of British Columbia towns to days-deep limits of wilderness as a fugitive from compromise, a self-contained presence.

The enhanced remoteness of given country here tends to convert its nature to alpine — a corollary to the grizzly's existence. If the earth weren't higher in some places than others, grizzlies wouldn't roam it. The grizzly needs very high earth of great extent — countless conifer trees, summer snow, barren green.

Over 10,000 grizzlies live in British Columbia, a land largely free of man-made alterations where alpine country and grizzlies constitute a dependable eco-cultural equation. The equation is operational at the high Coast Range pass that Route 99 attains between Pemberton Meadows and Lillooet. There, blue Joffre Glacier juts into the sky behind moss-draped fir trees, before the highway continues amidst lupine and indian paintbrush at the head of its hour-long descent into Lillooet.

Above 10k feet

Pull off of the road slightly beyond the glacier parking lot. Step into alpine, where silence and huge objects and distance present themselves. Snowy peaks appear in the sunlight. The country is too big to break down into hollow or cove or field or wood-lot, as with the East. It's too big to hurry out of if confused. The mind begins to work on it and accommodate it, but achieves only a certain degree of progress. Then the easterner's vacation ends and lesser country retakes the senses.

Hikers making the best use of available vacation time realize that the Joffre alpine terrain resolves the dilemma of those who find alpine territory imprac-tical to reach. Here, logging roads penetrate alpine and present it through a mere hour of walking. Though they pass through a disrupted landscape of harvested forest, they convey hikers above tree line and offer a route that ultimately transcends logging

I recall when hiking this trail pine and fir cones hanging about me in silent restatement of evergreen existence post-logging — Subalpine Fir cones, Douglas fir cones, Western White Pine cones along a timber road transformed into a luxury walkway with their multi-shaped adornment. Snow loomed mute on the peaks. Out of this static silence came the rushing of a mountain stream, drowning every sound along it — glacier water drawn from the melting silence. The rushing noise obscuring all other sound, I watched with greater attentiveness.

Logging cuts stretched for miles and miles, the heads and bodies of the trees looking down, the holes carved from the dragging burying me in a low-level forest of obstructions within great distances. So extensive is the ambiguity that the phrase "on your own" freshly asserts itself. Douglas fir trunks rose above the moss, a green meadow looming above the treetops; and, beyond, the noisy stream water. The grizzly's 120-square-mile home range was up there.

The grizzly's many miles are not a linear, flat route. Even if such were the case, the probability of an animal appearing within a few hundred yards of ground within a few moments of time would fore-stall a sighting for months, or even years. Grizzly country consists of rises and dips, tree trunks, branches, reducing sight to a level of fractionality that diminishes the odds of seeing a bear to nothing-ness. Lifetime woodsmen talk of occasions 20 years earlier when they saw a grizzly bear.

We are on our own, wondering about each step we take and whether it harmonizes with the envi-ronment to the extent necessary to finally bring a grizzly before us. Such circumstances breed differ-ent outlooks. We look to "instinct" and wonder if "it is time" for the country to show us one. Grizzly and man roam around looking for each other within this sharing of liberty.

Alone up there, we feel the need to associate ourselves with a creature greater than we are, an overseeing presence that, in its proximity, enlarges our view of self. I heard an acquaintance, his pack train of horses on a course to intersect a grizzly, tell of taking shelter behind the enhanced presence that the horses conveyed to the dominating animal. Another spoke of a sudden encounter, the grizzly's head three feet wide. Still in awe of the destructive potential of such an animal, their encounters embellish their lives and project their personal identities to others for a lifetime. For them, seeing their grizzly was a need fulfilled; those who have that need will likely see their grizzly because anticipation will sharpen their senses.

Some disrupt that process by paying a boat operator for an excursion to observe grizzlies feed on salmon behind Vancouver Island, where the Georgia Strait separates the island from the remote mainland of British Columbia. As dependably as lunching zoo bears, the grizzlies migrate from the wilderness to the shores of the strait.

I would hesitate to offer a fee to sever a years-long relationship between mountains and man yet ongoing with each anticipatory step in the silence. For me, it's enough to remember the grassy oval flattened out over 6 feet of clear-cut terrain near Joffre. I asked a British Columbia woodsman if that animal bed might have been made by a grizzly up in that territory and he told me it absolutely could have been. I had been in grizzly country.

Hike in twos or threes here. The weather reaches extremes, with a dusting of snow sometimes visible as early as September, presenting a hazard to a solitary hiker victimized by a health problem or an unexpected mountain lion or bear encounter. In 2011, a First Nations woman was killed and partially consumed by a bear near Lillooet.

CHAPTER 18

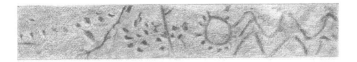

Mesa

SWEETWATER STATION, WYOMING

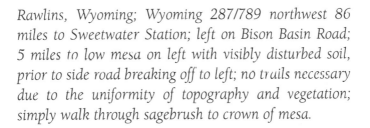

Rawlins, Wyoming; Wyoming 287/789 northwest 86 miles to Sweetwater Station; left on Bison Basin Road; 5 miles to low mesa on left with visibly disturbed soil, prior to side road breaking off to left; no trails necessary due to the uniformity of topography and vegetation; simply walk through sagebrush to crown of mesa.

The last gem I found was red — a transparent glow of red like the roots of a hemlock tree. The late afternoon sun lit my steps as they walked the long foot highway of a mesa littered with sun-shot stone. Millennia of wind had polished and worn their oranges and yellows and browns into wavy-shaped jewelry with unusual effects, like this red that appeared when angled sun struck the black surface.

Naturally shaped gems, each piece radically different than the next, caught my eye at every step, and I wondered what force distributed such abundance. Could it have been a violent earth movement breaking rock apart? Reflecting on my gems days later, I realized that a green forest bequeathed them to me.

They were agates, identifiable by their amber translucence when held to the sun, but organic agates formed of wood. Two hundred million years ago, the silicate mineral comprising agate infiltrated wood cells and replaced them, taking on their subtle colors of brownish-yellow, olive-brown, butterscotch and occasional root beer-red. The summit of the mesa was a long, agate-garnished forest tomb.

The forest stood two hundred million years ago — two hundred million years working a change that would transfer in an instant to my wife's eyes in a gift of agate earrings. Against this wind-blown backdrop, our temporal emotions and relations come into perspective and we realize that time makes all things whole and that philosophy is pointless. Like the other great areas of thought — finance, governance, religion, art — nature holds up endless time as a marker.

Nature presents us with insights that extend beyond science and into the realm of the mystical. Each human life senses patterns and parallels that answer the most troubling questions and set our days on course.

The colors in those wood agates paralleled colors over one thousand miles away amidst headwater springs of a forest at the crest of the Blue Ridge Mountains. There, reishi (*Ganoderma tsugae*) mushrooms protruded from dead hemlock trunks, taking on the same creamy orange, warm brown and root beer-red as they shone glossy in the humid summer.

Reishi grants the gift of medical healing through its cancer-mitigating effects; and for me, the give-and-take of friendship. Worth thousands of dollars when I marketed it to an Asian exporter, it answered my professional sponsorship of a friend from the remote highlands of the Philippines. Money had not been a consideration at the time; now, money grew freely from treetrunks. In nature is a giving back and forth for the aware.

Our desires are expressed through our searching eyes. For years I had gathered pebbles of red quartz but disqualified them as the gem rose quartz I lusted after because their red, from iron inclusions, merely stained the stone. Amid the scent of desert sagebrush on Sweetwater Mesa, I held a piece of quartz infused with pink within a dew-white exterior — rose quartz colored by an unknown agent, part of the rare and yet-to-be-known on Sweetwater Mesa.

There are thousands of Sweetwater Mesas in this sagebrush wilderness, and no limits to the new discoveries awaiting millions of new eyes. Gazing across that vast openness, nature asks what we want and tells us we will have it.

Water is the chief consideration of a hike here. The desert sun and wind, combined with the 6,500-foot altitude, drain a hiker without an adequate supply.

CHAPTER 19

Summit

SEQUOIA NATIONAL PARK, CALIFORNIA

(Mono Nation)

*Los Angeles, California; I5-N; 68 miles; CA-99; north
31 miles; CA-65-N; 65 miles; CA-198; east 43 miles.*

The road to the crowning path winds uphill in
hairpin curves for over 15 miles — over 6,
000 vertical feet — before the suite of defin-
itive Sequoia National Park trees appears, set in
solid rock at the crest of a granite cliff, a hiking path
fronting them in the mountain sun.

A few steps back amidst the conifers, a specimen
of the largest tree on earth stands laughing in the
shadows. No other tree approaches this giant
sequoia (*Sequoia gigantea*) in size. The thought
comes to mind that the 15 miles overseen by this
great natural entity reflect its dimensional achieve-
ment with some brilliance of their own, and the
rock-studded ascent affirms that notion.

Sequoia

Chalky white California sycamore trees (*Platanus racemosa*) frame a view of towering cliffs the pale tone of peeled bark, in a dialogue between rock and timber. Mountain mahogany trees shimmer in the sun as if living in an eternal spring.

Along the crowning trail, the Beetle Rock Trail, the lesser players in the forest shrink to smaller size in the demanding conditions, while the sequoia retains its gigantic dimensions. While the others become miniatures on the infertile surface of rock that forms the trail, striving for endurance in those stony holds, as befits a tree that has found immortality, it stands straight and broad as a vertical house.

These sequoias reflect immortal cheer on the valley floor far below. Rather than nondescript apple or peach orchards, there are sun-drenched flats brightened by golden lemons and oranges. The high country snow waters them with a rushing river that flows fresh even after months of rainless blue skies.

The function of these trees is to uplift us with their sunset-colored columns, and to inspire reverence for their form and great age. The First Nations people share such sentiments with the Europeans, who have felt them through a 175-year acquaintance with the species, but the sequoias have been here since before the coming of Columbus and fall of Rome.

They live for 5,000 years or more.

Such longevity amplifies their influence beyond basic forest ecology, possibly playing into larger climatic effects as a kind of botanical element. They mark a boundary between the dessicated ridges of southern California and forested Sierra to the north, and maybe they maintain that boundary with their fire resistance, promoting a long-term ecological scheme.

Culturally, these trees have lifted up the human race for thousands of years. Science admits that they do not perish from disease but simply topple over from their own weight. Maybe they are a statement from a glorious human past of Biblical people living for centuries. Maybe they are truly originals, inspiring us to live peacefully in high places as they do.

Take time to enjoy riverside swimming and picnicking along the waterfall-studded section of the Marble River running through the lower reaches of Sequoia National Park.

CHAPTER 20

Alpine Lava Flow

TIONESTA, CALIFORNIA

(Modoc Nation)

Alturas, California; CA-299; west 19 miles; CA-139; northwest 27 miles; CO. RD. 97; 7 miles; National Forest Road; 3 miles; wide spot on right at top of mountain.

The glass climax occurred along a National Forest road of ordinary dirt. Flecks of white pumice still litter the road banks, though only a geologist would translate the specks into evidence of the consummation. The plowed lanes roll beneath the car wheels. A sensuous tension holds terrain transcending high ground and approaching the bare essence of our planet.

Graded iron-rich red, the byway winds, a sun streak in a dark fir corridor. A tear in the forest fabric briefly reveals an absolute lapse of landscape —

an incident site — but the deep green soon closes the view as the corridor resumes the cooling approach to the spent surfaces — 6, 7,000 feet.

At the top, one of the road's flanks becomes a burnt heap and the other a steep mountain's foot. Here on Glass Mountain, California, Earth's hard hands, the casts of a volcanic eruption, are pitched to hold the white of snow in early July. In the mute disarray of the prostrate road flank, we have passed from the quiet of fir forest into the greater quiet of high fir forest and the still greater quiet of a landscape exhausted. Above a layer of forest fire smoke blended of burning fir trees and moss and pine needles, it is quieter than smoke. A primitive silence prevails 800 years after the Earth itself burned.

Along the brittle mannequin of the flank, the planet talks to the mind in random image-making. Objects stand at angles at which they should not stand, chipped and broken like the landscape surrounding them. Colors not proper for the light of the sun bake in sunlight. In piles of gleaming black obsidian, the Earth itself laughs out of turn, a calming laugh, enduring, from deep within itself, and we see the bright smile of stone.

The hike here is self-directed, an inner walk. Bereft of signage, it branches off into wreckage to explore variations of wreckage. Within a crunching obsidian passageway, the eye picks up signals from travelers who place objects along the trail edge to maintain their sense of direction through the 4210 acres of undefined debris.

The hike traverses a geologic smile of unifying happiness. As the hiker's hours pass inside Earth in this pure air, at a high elevation removed from people and the carbon-laden forest atmospherics, light visits him. This fresh light increasing, the eyes, from pondering this dimension of new creation, squint into a distance that takes in the Blue Ridges, the Canadian Rockies, the Smokies, the Atlantic coast, the Pacific coast. Fragrance reaches the light from the smoke layer below arising seemingly from a new Earth still burning. The evidence of creative force unifies East and West, Appalachian and Sierra.

After the AD 1200 eruption, initial life presents itself in bright flashes, like flowers in a vase, to memorialize the great event. Pink Alpine penstemon (*Penstemon davidsonii*) creeps low over the obsidian. A mountain bluebird with hardly a branch to land on flies across the barrenness with the color of pure, clear sky on its back, toward a cluster of whitebark pine (*Pinus albicaulis*) laboring to find nourishment in the incipient earthscape. The sky returns the Earth's smile. When sun touches certain grades of the obsidian, rainbows appear on the slick surface; the blue of summer sky glosses other grades.

Across the road on the overseeing mountainside, an intact high ground landscape rises in an even geometry drawn over thousands of years, its angle offset with the straight lines of tree trunks. Past a snow patch and into the firs and spruces, the ever-green trunks are erect and broad, and sun beams light silence. This is a giant den, with trees to lean back against, soft needles underfoot, fragrant wood smoke during the summer fire season. Chunks of obsidian glow like charcoal in the sunny places.

A spiritual mirage overwhelms the diversity of destinations and limitations of distance. A spreading smile invites our footsteps, leads to the eloquent dignity of moss-hung tree trunks and sun-patched silence.

This silent influence led me onward to a high place where this Earth happiness stretches along the roadside like perpetual gleaming snow heaped up. It was a raven's flight away from Glass Mountain, where a smiling native woman, keeper of a post office and of road directions through the nearby wilderness, showed me the dirt road to the Earth smile, after a cowboy with a border collie and his hired hand pointed her out as I ate lunch.

When I found the place she guided me to, I saw that the tree trunks there were statuesque, their boughs stately; stumps from long-ago logging showed the elevated memorials of cedars, pines, fir in the shadow-sunlight of deep forest.

Here on the summit of Buck Mountain, above Davis Creek, the exploding lava cooled fastest, first lava out of the Earth, producing a pure obsidian like polished black iron that shone gem-like, some with mahogany mapped out within the black in dialogue with the brown conifer trunks. On how many mantles and desks does it shine; in years past, on the tips of how many First Nations bows?

I stood beside our car, in its trunk a bright harvest of the obsidian, far above an empty valley studded with sagebrush, beyond pastures and through dust to this place, its recognition initiated by First Nations people foraging material for arrowheads, then extended by obsidian miners. The cowboy pulled his truck to a stop within the evergreen shadows and asked if I had found what I wanted, and I returned his smile. Later, I read that native people characterized the country around Buck Mountain as "the smiles of God."

The drive back down led into quiet places of wind and bird song; yet, behind me, there was a higher silence.

Check with Lava Beds National Monument for road conditions before ascending to Glass Mountain, as snow often blocks the way even in summer.

Epilogue

High in the Medicine Bow Mountains, there is no parched summer of a water-challenged world. Up there in the clouds, golden arnica (*Arnica cordifolia*) flowers stud the fir needles and amythest Calypso orchids (*Calypso bulbosa*) people a grassy spring granted by the moisture that graces this closer proximity to eternity. A planetary entity, calypso orchid displays from Wyoming to Russia to New England its almost personal need for quiet seclusion.

Across the miles-wide valley in the Snowy Range, acres of golden glacier lilies (*Erythronium grandiflorum*) brighten white snowbanks, amidst life surging in the melting white moisture. Big columbine flowers (*Aquilegia caerulea*) burst out like daffodils in a garden. Blue flowers, pink flowers —

over a dozen kinds brighten the ground with the colors of an Easter egg hunt.

Here in these heights is an earthly functionality. At the highest year-round cabin in the Medicine Bows, 9640 feet, solar panels harvest the intense sunlight. A spring begins to flow downslope into a gravity-fed kitchen sink, then a zinc bathtub and the gathering of calypso orchids before it descends in the direction of the southeast-northwest flight path and its planes following each other amidst midnight quartz chips above this vast territory of Christmas trees.

We strive for this basic functionality in order to survive. At Medicine Bow Camp, the water-wasting lawnmower highway ends. Colorful stone from diverse places xeriscapes the drive. The high ground quartzite and granite stones are a chronology of pretty places and pretty days, in step with man and Earth.

About the Author

Bill Rozday works at a globally known financial information firm in Washington, D.C. but says his most productive years were those spent building and hiking a path into a western Pennsylvania "hollow." *"It showed me that money, like everything, is a long path up and down, through seasons."*

His "unemployment" has been followed by a busy life of travel, but that ribbon of dirt beneath the trees still means as much as subsequent hikes in glacial British Columbia and the California desert. *"My path was ground zero of equality and joy in living."*

Made in the USA
Middletown, DE
11 May 2015